THE **BILL** OF **RIGHTS**

Roberta Baxter

Heinemann
LIBRARY

Chicago, Illinois

www.capstonepub.com
Visit our website to find out more information about Heinemann-Raintree books.

To order:
☎ Phone 800-747-4992
💻 Visit www.capstonepub.com
to browse our catalog and order online.

Edited by Abby Colich, Megan Cotugno, and Laura Hensley
Designed by Cynthia Della-Rovere
Original illustrations © Capstone Global Library Limited 2011
Illustrated by Oxford Designers & Illustrators
Picture research by Tracy Cummins
Originated by Capstone Global Library Limited
Printed and bound in the United States of America in Eau Claire, Wisconsin. 072013 007600RP

16 15 14 13
10 9 8 7 6 5 4 3

Library of Congress Cataloging-in-Publication Data
Baxter, Roberta, 1952-
 The Bill of Rights / Roberta Baxter.
  p. cm.—(Documenting U.S. history)
 Includes bibliographical references and index.
 ISBN 978-1-4329-6751-2 (hb)—ISBN 978-1-4329-6760-4 (pb) 1. United States. Constitution. 1st-10th Amendments—Juvenile literature. 2. Civil rights—United States—History—Juvenile literature. 3. Constitutional history—United States—Juvenile literature. I. Title.
 KF4749.B35 2013
 342.7308'5—dc23   2011037780

Acknowledgments
The author and publishers are grateful to the following for permission to reproduce copyright material: Alamy: pp. 4 (© Visions of America, LLC), 29 (© North Wind Picture Archives), 30 (© Michael Matthews - Police Images); Corbis: pp. 12 (© Francis G. Mayer), 19 (© Bettmann), 20 (© Ocean), 25 (© JLP/Jose L. Pelaez); Getty Images: pp. 7 (Alex Wong), 17 (The Bridgeman Art Library), 33 (Andrew Gombert-Pool), 43 (Scott J. Ferrell/ Congressional Quarterly); Library of Congress Prints and Photographs Division: pp. 9, 10, 11, 13, 14, 16, 26; National Archives: pp. 21, 37, 38; Shutterstock: pp. 6 (© Ben Shafer), 27 (© Ryan Rodrick Beiler), 35 (© Ryan Rodrick Beiler), 41 top (© Konstantin L); US Mint: p. 41 bottom.

Cover image of Thomas Jefferson reproduced with permission from the Library of Congress Prints and Photographs Division. Cover image of James Madison reproduced with permission from the Library of Congress Prints and Photographs Division. Cover image of the Bill of Rights reproduced with permission from the National Archives (Charters of Freedom).

Every effort has been made to contact copyright holders of material reproduced in this book. Any omissions will be rectified in subsequent printings if notice is given to the publisher.

Contents

Some words are printed in **bold**, like this. You can find out what they mean by looking in the glossary.

Important Documents

We learn about history through evidence left by people from the past. Letters, diaries, photographs, newspapers, and published documents tell us the story of the people who lived through the events of history. They explain how people lived and worked, and what they thought.

Primary sources

Primary sources include words written by people in the past. They can include published documents such as newspapers and government papers. They can also be letters, diaries, or notes from meetings. Some primary sources are not written down at all. Clothes, furniture, and other original objects are also examples of primary sources. Historians study all these things to learn what a time period was like or what people were thinking.

The Bill of Rights is one of the most important primary sources in the United States. Its authors put forward some of the core values of the new country. The Bill of Rights helped define the basic rights of U.S. citizens. People still refer back to it today to help define the rights of all Americans.

Secondary sources

Secondary sources also help people learn about history. They include documents written about history—but by writers who did not actually experience the events. Rather, these authors have studied primary sources and then written about the subject at a later time. Textbooks are an example of a secondary source. Historians always prefer to rely on primary sources in their research. But secondary sources can also be important.

Primary sources help people learn about the past.

The original Bill of Rights, along with many other important historical documents, are kept in the National Archives building in Washington, D.C.

Preserving original documents

Original documents must be preserved and protected so that future generations can see these primary sources. The Library of **Congress**, in Washington, D.C., has more than 147 million items from U.S. history, including books, maps, photographs, and videos. It is the largest library in the world. It is open to members of Congress and to the American people.

The National **Archives** and Records Administration, in Washington, D.C., also stores valuable historical documents. It manages all national records and contains many important documents, letters, diaries, and photographs.

The National Archives contains the three most important documents in U.S. history: the Bill of Rights, the **Declaration of Independence**, and the **Constitution**.

Known together as the Charters of Freedom, they are displayed in a rotunda (round room). More than one million visitors see the Charters of Freedom every year.

Protecting original documents

Original documents are protected in fireproof boxes, and the temperature and humidity (moisture in the air) are carefully controlled. Paper can darken and ink can fade away, so the boxes are made of materials that will protect the documents. Other documents, such as the Bill of Rights, are written on **parchment**, a kind of leather. Parchment must be kept at the right moisture level so that it will not be destroyed.

Many important documents are locked away. The ones on display, such as the Charters of Freedom, are guarded during the times that the public can view them. The history of the United States is told through these documents and objects, so they must be carefully protected.

Guards stand near the National Archive's display of the Bill of Rights in Washington, D.C.

We Need a Bill of Rights!

In 1783 the United States was a brand-new country. It had just won the struggle against Great Britain known as the **Revolutionary War** (1775–1783). The 13 original **colonies** had won their independence and could now rule themselves. But how would they be governed?

The Articles of Confederation

At first, the laws governing the young country came from a document called the Articles of Confederation. But the Articles did not work well. Each state made its own rules. **Congress** could not tax the people to pay for the government. There was no president, and the country was run by committees.

The Constitutional Convention

To resolve these problems, a group of **delegates** from the new states held a meeting called the Constitutional **Convention**. Fifty-five leaders came to Independence Hall in Philadelphia, Pennsylvania, starting on May 14, 1787. They worked for four months.

After much discussion, the delegates agreed to throw away the Articles of Confederation and work on a new document— the **Constitution**.

1775–1783
The Revolutionary War is fought in America.

1783
After the American colonies declare victory, they are governed by the Articles of Confederation.

To balance power, the delegates designed a government with three branches, or parts:

- The legislative (lawmaking) branch is made up of the Congress.

- The executive branch is made up of the president and vice president.

- The judicial branch is made up of the Supreme Court.

All three branches have powers to stop the actions of the others. This system is known as checks and balances. It prevents any one branch from becoming too powerful. The first words of the Constitution show where the main power would be: "We, the people..."

Know It!

Rhode Island refused to send delegates to the Constitutional Convention. Its delegates thought a constitution would weaken their state.

The Constitutional Convention was held in this building.

May 14, 1787
The Constitutional Convention meets in Philadelphia and works on the Constitution.

Making the Constitution law

In order for the Constitution to become law, at least 9 of the 13 states had to **ratify**, or approve, it. Most delegates were not happy with every detail of the document. Some delegates, like George Mason from Virginia, thought there should also be a bill of rights. A bill of rights is a document that lists all the rights and privileges of the people in a nation. Instead, the Constitution focused more on how the government would be run. Still, many delegates agreed that the Constitution was a good start and should be approved.

"I confess that there are several parts of this Constitution which I do not at present approve. But I am not sure I shall never approve them."
—Ben Franklin

Ben Franklin helped compose many important documents in United States history.

Protect our rights

But as the convention delegates returned home, controversy erupted about the lack of a bill of rights. People remembered that their rights as British citizens were once taken away by Great Britain. Just before the Revolutionary War began, the British **Parliament** passed a series of unfair taxes. The **colonists** had no representatives in Parliament to argue against these taxes.

To make themselves heard, the colonists dumped a British ship's supply of tea into Boston Harbor. Parliament reacted by closing the port and sending in more soldiers.

In response to British actions, the colonists fought and won their independence. Now that they had their own country, they did not want the new U.S. government to be powerful enough to take away their rights once again.

Colonists responded to British rule by dumping a British ship's supply of tea into Boston Harbor. This event became known as the Boston Tea Party.

1787
The delegates of the Constitutional Convention return home to get the states to ratify the Constitution. They find there is opposition to the lack of a bill of rights.

Federalists vs. Anti-Federalists

In each state, men were chosen to attend ratifying conventions. Here, people could discuss any problems they had with the Constitution. There was much debate. People called **Federalists** believed that no bill of rights was needed in the Constitution. Meanwhile, **Anti-Federalists** thought a bill of rights was essential to limit the power of the federal (national) government and protect the rights of individuals.

"The Federalist Papers"

Representing the Federalist point of view, a collection of essays known as "The Federalist Papers" was published in New York newspapers by **Founding Fathers** Alexander Hamilton and James Madison. These essays argued that the Constitution should be ratified. They argued that no bill of rights was necessary because the Constitution says, "We, the people." This leaves the power of the government in the hands of the citizens, they argued.

Alexander Hamilton (about 1755–1804)

Alexander Hamilton fought in the Revolutionary War. After the war, he became a strong Federalist and wrote many of the essays in "The Federalist Papers." He later became the nation's first Secretary of the Treasury.

October 1787–August 1788
"The Federalist Papers" are published. The authors argue in favor of ratifying the Constitution.

Disagreements

Not everyone agreed with this argument. For example, Patrick Henry of Virginia refused to sign the Constitution. He said it needed a bill of rights. Henry felt that without a bill of rights, the president could act like a king. He wanted to limit the power of the federal government.

Patrick Henry (1736–1799)

Patrick Henry (standing in center) was a leader during the Revolutionary War who became famous for his "Give me Liberty, or give me Death!" speech. After the war, Henry became a strong Anti-Federalist. In his home state of Virginia, he fought against the ratification of the Constitution. He twice served as the governor of Virginia.

June 1788
Patrick Henry, of Virginia, argues against ratifying the Constitution.

Know It!

The Constitution of the United States is the oldest written constitution still in effect in the world today.

Compromise

James Madison of Virginia played a big part in shaping the Constitution. At first he opposed the idea of a bill of rights. He felt that the Constitution's division of power among the three branches of government (see page 9) would be enough to protect individual rights. At the same time, Madison did not want the Constitution to fail to be ratified because of the lack of a bill of rights.

Then, in December 1787, Madison received a letter from Thomas Jefferson, who was serving as ambassador (representative for the United States) in France. Jefferson wrote to Madison: "A bill of rights is what the people are entitled to against every government on earth." Madison came to decide that a bill of rights was a good compromise to get the Constitution ratified. He promised that he would work for a bill of rights when the new government began.

Thomas Jefferson insisted that the United States needed a bill of rights.

Ratifying the Constitution

At last, the ratifying conventions of the states voted, one by one, to approve the Constitution (see the chart). By June 1788, the Constitution had been ratified. But many of the state conventions added a list of **amendments** to be included in a future bill of rights. For many people, they only agreed to ratify the Constitution with the understanding that a bill of rights was to come.

Ratification of the Constitution	
State	**Date**
Delaware	December 7, 1787
Pennsylvania	December 12, 1787
New Jersey	December 18, 1787
Georgia	January 2, 1788
Connecticut	January 9, 1788
Massachusetts	February 6, 1788
Maryland	April 28, 1788
South Carolina	May 23, 1788
New Hampshire	June 21, 1788
Virginia	June 25, 1788
New York	July 26, 1788
North Carolina	November 21, 1789
Rhode Island	May 29, 1790

December 1787
Thomas Jefferson encourages James Madison to consider a bill of rights.

June 1788
The Constitution is ratified by nine states.

The New Government Begins

In March 1789, the new U.S. government met in Federal Hall in New York City. George Washington was sworn in as the first president of the United States on April 30, 1789.

Madison's promise

James Madison was elected to the **House of Representatives**, representing Virginia. In his new role, he remembered his promise to work on a bill of rights. On May 4, 1789, Madison made a speech, asking the House to consider a bill of rights.

Many members of **Congress** thought Madison should wait until other important matters were settled. But Madison continued his push.

Federal Hall in New York City, shown here, is where the first U.S. government met.

March 1789
The first U.S. government meets in Federal Hall, in New York City.

April 30, 1789
George Washington is sworn in as the first president of the United States.

James Madison
(1751–1836)

James Madison was only 5 feet, 4 inches (1.6 meters) tall and weighed 100 pounds (45 kilograms). He was often sick and had a weak voice. When he spoke in Congress, many had trouble hearing him. Still, Madison's words made a huge difference in the future of the country, as he played a big role in creating both the **Constitution** and the Bill of Rights. Madison went on to be the fourth president of the United States, serving from 1809 to 1817.

On June 8, he spoke about the importance of the issue. His speech was published in newspapers, and many citizens approved of his ideas.

On July 21, Madison proposed a list of rights, including many the states had requested. He built on the **Declaration of Independence**, written by Thomas Jefferson, and the Virginia Declaration of Rights, written by George Mason. He also referred to the Magna Carta, a document from 1215 that had established rights for British citizens.

June 8, 1789
James Madison speaks in Congress about the importance of a bill of rights.

July 21, 1789
Madison proposes a list of rights, forming the basis of the Bill of Rights.

Amendments chosen

A group called the Committee of Eleven, made up of one person from each state represented in Congress at the time, met to consider **amendments**. (North Carolina and Rhode Island had not yet **ratified** the Constitution, so those two states were not represented.)

Congress received 100 amendments from the states' ratifying **conventions**. Madison compiled these along with his own into a list for the Committee of Eleven. It was decided that any new rights and changes would be added as amendments, not into the text of the Constitution. The Committee recommended the amendments to the House of Representatives. On August 24, 1789, the House of Representatives debated and then approved 17 amendments.

June–July 1789
The Committee of Eleven meets for the first time to consider amendments to the Constitution.

August 24, 1789
The House of Representatives debates and approves 17 amendments to the Constitution.

This illustration shows the signing of the U.S. Constitution.

Amendments printed

A man named Thomas Greenleaf (see the box) printed these amendments, and the copies were sent to the Senate. Some senators felt the issue of the amendments should come after other important work. But they took about two weeks to consider them. The Senate made some changes and ended up with 12 amendments.

Finally, a committee of both representatives and senators worked out a list of 12 amendments. It was hoped that these would be passed to form a final bill of rights.

August 1789
Thomas Greenleaf prints the recommended amendments. The Senate approves a list of 12 amendments.

To the States

On September 25, 1789, **Congress** passed the 12 **amendments** and gave them to President Washington.

Engrossed copies

William Lambert, a congressional clerk, **engrossed** a copy of the amendments for each state. He wrote the words on **parchment** (see the box). The words were written in a fancy style called calligraphy. The pen used was a quill—a feather from a duck or goose. When a quill was dipped into an inkwell, the ink rose up inside the hollow feather. A person could write several words before dipping the quill again.

A quill and inkwell are shown here with a copy of the Bill of Rights.

September 25, 1789
Congress passes 12 amendments and gives them to President Washington.

October 2, 1789
A copy of the amendments and a letter from President Washington are sent to each state for consideration.

Know It!

Parchment comes from the skin of a sheep, calf, or goat. The hair is scraped off and the skin is stretched and dried. It becomes a thin, flexible piece of leather and lasts for a long time. We still have original copies of the amendments because of the endurance of parchment.

Amendments signed and sent out

Four people signed the amendments: Speaker of the House Frances Muhlenberg; President of the Senate John Adams; Secretary of the Senate Samuel Otis; and Clerk of the House John Beckley.

A copy of the amendments and a letter from President Washington were sent to each state. Based on the law established by Article V of the **Constitution**, three-fourths of the states had to **ratify** the amendments before they became law. Then, they would become the first amendments to the Constitution—a bill of rights.

The Bill of Rights is the first 12 amendments of the U.S. Constitution.

What was the content of the two amendments that were not passed? Amendment I stated that there should be one representative for every 30,000 people and no more than 200 representatives. Amendment II said that members of Congress could not vote themselves a pay raise until after an election. Amendment II was later passed as Amendment XXVII in 1992.

The process of ratification

As secretary of state, Thomas Jefferson kept track of which of the 12 amendments were approved or not approved by each state. Amendments III through XII were eventually ratified, but the first two amendments were not approved by enough of the states (see the box).

By the end of 1791, the United States was made up of 14 states. (Vermont was added to the original 13 states in 1791.) So 11 states would now have to ratify the amendments. On December 15, 1791, Virginia became the 11th state to ratify 10 of the amendments (see the chart). These 10 amendments would form the Bill of Rights.

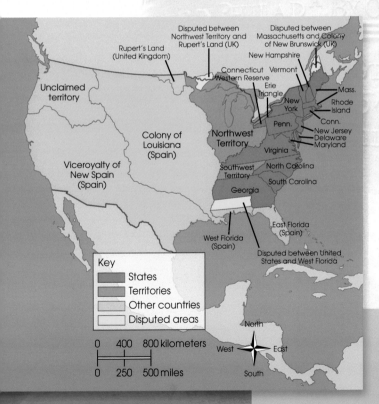

Key
- States
- Territories
- Other countries
- Disputed areas

0 400 800 kilometers
0 250 500 miles

This map shows the states that made up the United States in 1791. The land that makes up the rest of the continental United States today was claimed by many different groups at that time.

Ratification of the Bill of Rights		
State	**Date**	**Amendments approved**
New Jersey	November 20, 1789	Rejected Amendment II
Maryland	December 19, 1789	Approved all
North Carolina	December 22, 1789	Approved all
South Carolina	January 19, 1790	Approved all
New Hampshire	January 25, 1790	Rejected Amendment II
Delaware	January 28, 1790	Rejected Amendment I
New York	February 24, 1790	Rejected Amendment II
Pennsylvania	March 10, 1790	Rejected Amendment II
Rhode Island	May 29, 1790	Rejected Amendment II
Vermont	November 3, 1791	Approved all
Virginia	December 15, 1791	Approved all

December 15, 1791
Virginia becomes the 11th state to ratify the 10 amendments that become the Bill of Rights. This gives the amendments enough support to become law.

The First Three Amendments

The 10 **amendments** that were **ratified** became the Bill of Rights we know today. Many of these amendments developed out of the conditions before the **Revolutionary War**. People had seen their rights violated, and they wanted to be sure this never happened again.

Freedom of religion

In the 1600s, the Pilgrims and other early settlers came to North America to worship as they pleased. In England, they were not allowed to attend their own church, and they were forced to support the Church of England.

> "**Congress** shall make no law respecting an establishment of religion, or prohibiting the free exercise thereof..."
>
> —*The First Amendment*

The First Amendment (see box) states that the government cannot establish a national religion, and it must let all citizens choose to worship or not worship as they wish. Under the protection of the First Amendment, everyone can practice their religion with their own beliefs. A person who has no religion is also protected.

Controversy over the First Amendment

Since the Bill of Rights was passed, the boundaries of the First Amendment have been tested, especially in schools. People who worship as Jehovah's Witnesses feel that saluting the flag goes against their beliefs. In 1943, the U.S. Supreme Court ruled that students of the Jehovah's Witness faith do not have to salute the flag or say the "Pledge of Allegiance."

When people objected to daily prayers recited by students in public school, the U.S. Supreme Court ruled that the organized classroom prayers had to stop. Students were still allowed to gather for prayers if they wanted, but forcing all to pray the same prayer was against the First Amendment.

Many U.S. students say the Pledge of Allegiance every day.

25

> "[Congress shall make no law]... abridging [taking away] the freedom of speech, or of the press; or the right of the people to peaceably assemble, and to petition the Government for a redress [setting right] of grievances [complaints]."
>
> —*The First Amendment*

Freedom of speech

In the American **colonies**, citizens and newspaper publishers had been jailed for criticizing the royal governor or the king. The Bill of Rights ensured that would not happen again.

Martin Luther King, Jr.
(1929–1968)

Throughout U.S. history, many people have bravely used their First Amendment rights. In the 1960s, African Americans fought for equal treatment and rights. The Reverend Martin Luther King, Jr. was a leader of this **civil rights** movement. He was a powerful speaker, and he used words and large-scale gatherings to inspire people to action. He delivered his famous "I Have a Dream" speech during a march in Washington, D.C., for civil rights. He was later assassinated (murdered) for his beliefs.

The First Amendment (see box) also provides for freedom of speech and freedom of the press (meaning reporting in places such as newspapers). Under the First Amendment, people can speak or write what they believe. But they cannot say or write something that is false and destroys a person's reputation. It is also illegal to say or write something that is obscene (offensive) or tell secrets that would damage national security.

The right to assemble and protest

The First Amendment also gives the right to assemble and **protest** peacefully against the government. If an assembly becomes violent, the police can stop it. But citizens can march or protest against a policy that they dislike.

The First Amendment allows for freedom of assembly. This means people can gather publicly to demonstrate their beliefs.

The Second Amendment

Militias were groups of citizen soldiers who used their guns to protect their communities in the American colonies and then the early United States. The Second Amendment (see box) mentions a militia. The second part of the amendment says that the people have the right to own firearms, or guns.

Some people believe the right to own firearms was meant to be only for those who are soldiers. But others think it means that anyone can own a gun. The wording can be interpreted in different ways. When the Bill of Rights was written, most people had guns for protection and for hunting for food. Most experts today say the amendment means that anyone who is not a criminal can own a gun if they choose. Others disagree.

> "A well regulated Militia, being necessary to the security of a free State, the right of the people to keep and bear Arms, shall not be infringed [taken away]."
>
> —*The Second Amendment*

The Third Amendment

In 1768, before the Revolutionary War, 4,000 British soldiers came to Boston. The **colonists** there were forced to allow the soldiers to live in their houses, which was called quartering. The **Declaration of Independence** listed this situation (quartering) as one of the ways that Britain's King George III had taken away the rights of the people. The Third Amendment (see box) made sure this would never happen again.

"No Soldier shall, in time of peace be quartered in any house, without the consent of the Owner, nor in time of war, but in a manner to be prescribed by law."

—*The Third Amendment*

British soldiers are shown forcing their way into these colonists' home.

The Bill of Rights and the Court System

A large part of the Bill of Rights is dedicated to protecting people's rights within the court system.

The Fourth Amendment

According to the Fourth **Amendment** (see box), police cannot search a person's home or take a person's possessions without a reason. They must receive permission from a judge for the search or seizure (taking).

"The right of the people to be secure in their persons, houses, papers, and effects, against unreasonable searches and seizures, shall not be violated, and no Warrants shall issue, but upon probable cause, supported by Oath or affirmation, and particularly describing the place to be searched, and the persons or things to be seized."

—*The Fourth Amendment*

Police officers need permission from a judge to search someone's home.

The Fifth Amendment

The Fifth Amendment (see box) gives citizens rights when they are accused of a crime. They are innocent until proven guilty. They also cannot be tried for the same crime twice.

"No person shall be held to answer for a capital [requiring the death penalty], or otherwise infamous [major] crime, unless on a presentment or indictment [formal charge] of a Grand Jury, except in cases arising in the land or naval forces, or in the Militia, when in actual service in time of War or public danger; nor shall any person be subject for the same offence to be twice put in jeopardy of life or limb; nor shall be compelled in any criminal case to be a witness against himself, nor be deprived of life, liberty, or property, without due process of law; nor shall private property be taken for public use, without just compensation [payment]."

—*The Fifth Amendment*

The Sixth Amendment

The Sixth Amendment (see box) is also about trials and courts. According to the Sixth Amendment, a person has the right to a speedy trial, to gather witnesses, and to know exactly what crime he or she is accused of. People accused of a crime are provided a defense lawyer if they cannot afford one.

"In all criminal prosecutions, the accused shall enjoy the right to a speedy and public trial, by an impartial [open-minded] jury of the State and district wherein the crime shall have been committed, which district shall have been previously ascertained [confirmed] by law, and to be informed of the nature and cause of the accusation; to be confronted with the witnesses against him; to have compulsory [required] process for obtaining witnesses in his favor, and to have the Assistance of Counsel [a lawyer] for his defense.

—*The Sixth Amendment*

Persons in the United States accused of a crime have the right to a fair and speedy trial.

The Seventh Amendment

The Seventh Amendment (see box) says that if a large amount of money ($20 in 1791) is involved, a person can ask for a jury trial. Although this amount is too little for a lawsuit today, the government has not changed the amendment.

"In suits at common law, where the value in controversy shall exceed twenty dollars, the right of trial by jury shall be preserved, and no fact tried by a jury, shall be otherwise re-examined in any court of the United States, than according to the rules of the common law."

—*The Seventh Amendment*

The Eighth Amendment

The Eighth Amendment (see box) states that excessive (overly high) bail cannot be charged for a person accused of a crime to get out of jail until trial. It also prohibits "cruel and unusual punishment." Some have said this made the death penalty illegal, but the U.S. Supreme Court has ruled it is not.

> "Excessive bail shall not be required, nor excessive fines imposed, nor cruel and unusual punishments inflicted."
>
> —*The Eighth Amendment*

The Ninth Amendment

According to the Ninth Amendment (see box), other rights beyond those listed in the **Constitution** exist and should be respected. It would be impossible to list every right that a person might have or need, and so this amendment was meant to establish that other rights are also protected.

> "The enumeration [listing] in the Constitution, of certain rights, shall not be construed [interpreted] to deny or disparage [disrespect] others retained by the people."
>
> —*The Ninth Amendment*

"The powers not delegated to the United States by the Constitution, nor prohibited by it to the States, are reserved to the States respectively, or to the people."

—*The Tenth Amendment*

The Tenth Amendment

The Tenth Amendment (see box) gives all powers not given to the federal government to the states. By dividing power among the people, the state governments, and the federal government, the creators of the Bill of Rights hoped to create checks and balances. That way, no one would have too much power.

In the United States, the people have the power to come together to make change happen.

Protecting the Document

As one of the United States' most important documents, the copy of the Bill of Rights displayed in the National **Archives** receives special treatment.

Copies conserved

Before the Bill of Rights was placed on display, **conservators** carefully examined it. They looked at it through a microscope to make sure that there were no loose flakes of ink. They mended small tears with special paper and paste.

Know It!

In 1789, 14 states received an **engrossed** copy of the Bill of Rights. The copy sent to North Carolina was stolen by a Union soldier during the Civil War (1861–1865). After the war, the document was sold several times and then offered for sale to North Carolina. The state refused to buy what belonged to it. In 2005 the FBI got the copy and returned it to the state government of North Carolina. It had been missing from the state for 140 years.

Know It!

For years, one of the copies of the Bill of Rights was stored with other government records in the State Department. Then it was moved to the National Archives.

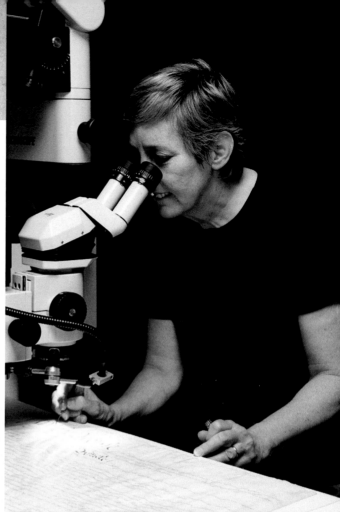

This conservator, Catherine Nicholson, uses a microscope to carefully restore a document.

In 2003 the Bill of Rights was placed into a special sealed box so it could be displayed. Light levels are kept low, to keep the ink from fading. The gas inside of the box is something called argon instead of air. This protects the document from chemical damage caused by oxygen in air. Temperature and humidity (moisture in the air) are kept low to help preserve the Bill of Rights for hundreds of years into the future.

2003
The Bill of Rights is placed into a special sealed box so it can be displayed at the National Archives in Washington, D.C.

Archivist of the United States

An **archivist** works to collect, preserve, and display important historical items, such as letters, diaries, notes, films, and videos. Most archivists work in museums. But one person holds the title of Archivist of the United States.

In 2009 President Barack Obama appointed David S. Ferriero to be the 10th Archivist of the United States. Ferriero works at the National Archives to protect the records of our country. When asked what his favorite part of the job is, he says: "Getting to see the various records for which I am responsible—more than 10 billion pieces of paper, 40 million photographs, miles and miles of film and video, and terabytes of electronic information."

David S. Ferriero's job is to oversee the National Archives, the organization that keeps records of all important U.S. historical documents.

Know It!

When the Bill of Rights was written, the person used **parchment**, quills, and ink. Now, the debates and procedures of **Congress** are recorded and published daily. Much of the discussion can be seen on television.

If you would like to be an archivist, Ferriero recommends that you: "Read a lot of history! Spend a lot of time in your library. Get to know your librarians—you can learn a lot from them. Start documenting your own family history—ask your parents and grandparents what they remember about their parents and grandparents. Write it down. Look for photographs that might be around the house and add those to your histories. You are starting your own family archive!"

The Bill of Rights Today

The Bill of Rights still works for Americans today. If there is a question about people's rights, it may be settled by the Supreme Court. The interaction between the American people and their government is still balanced by the Bill of Rights.

Rights for all

When the Bill of Rights was written, it protected the rights of the people who could vote at the time—which only included white men. Women could not vote, and most black people were slaves. American Indians were not thought of as citizens. So the Bill of Rights did not apply to everybody.

In 1870 the 15th **Amendment** to the **Constitution** gave every man, regardless of race or color, the right to vote. In 1920 the 19th Amendment gave women the right to vote. American Indians came to be thought of as equal Americans. The Bill of Rights finally applied to all citizens.

Responsibilities

Many citizens of the United States are proud of their country's laws. But with the privileges of the Bill of Rights come responsibilities. Citizens must be on guard to protect the rights of everyone.

The United States Supreme Court Building is shown here. The Supreme Court judges make decisions regarding the rights of Americans.

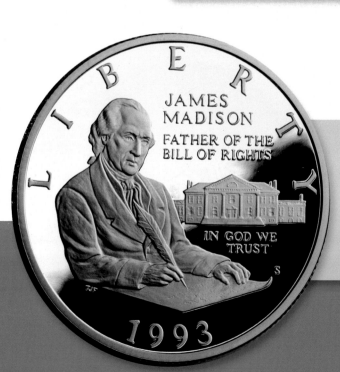

James Madison is commemorated on this silver half dollar as the father of the Bill of Rights.

Leaders' comments

Throughout history, the leaders of the United States have known how important the Bill of Rights is to freedom. Take a look at the quotations on these two pages to see what important U.S. citizens have said about the Bill of Rights. Now it is up to you to understand and protect these important rights for the future!

"A Bill of Rights is what the people are entitled to against every government on earth...and what no just government should refuse."

—*Thomas Jefferson, author of the* **Declaration of Independence** *and third president of the United States*

"[The Bill of Rights is] very important to...personal security, which is so truly characteristic of a free Government."

—*John Hancock, signer of the Declaration of Independence and governor of Massachusetts*

"Those who deny freedom to others do not deserve it for themselves."

—*Abraham Lincoln, 16th president of the United States*

"The Bill of Rights, contained in the first ten amendments to the Constitution, is every American's guarantee of freedom."

—*Harry S. Truman, 33rd president of the United States*

Capt. Kurt White　Prof. Robert C. Clark　Hon. Gregory Garre　Prof. Ronald Rotunda　Robert Alt　Ed Whelan　Prof. Stephen Press

*Centuries later, the government of the **Founding Fathers** is still in action today.*

"We were the first people in history to found a nation on the basis of individual rights."

—*Warren E. Burger, justice (judge) of the Supreme Court*

"America must remain freedom's staunchest [strongest] friend, for freedom is our best ally."

—*Ronald Reagan, 40th president of the United States*

Know It!

In 1941 President Franklin D. Roosevelt declared December 15 as Bill of Rights Day. That is the day that Virginia **ratified** the **amendments** and made the document official. In 2011 the Bill of Rights turned 220 years old.

"As a man is said to have a right to his property, he may be equally said to have a property in his rights."

—*James Madison, "father" of the Bill of Rights and fourth president of the United States*

Timeline

1775–1783

The Revolutionary War is fought in America.

1783

After the American colonies declare victory, they are governed by the Articles of Confederation.

June 1788

The Constitution is ratified by nine states.

June 1788

Patrick Henry, of Virginia, argues against ratifying the Constitution.

March 1789

The first U.S. government meets in Federal Hall, in New York City.

April 30, 1789

George Washington is sworn in as the first president of the United States.

September 25, 1789

Congress passes 12 amendments and gives them to President Washington.

August 1789

Thomas Greenleaf prints the recommended amendments. The Senate approves a list of 12 amendments.

October 2, 1789

A copy of the amendments and a letter from President Washington are sent to each state for consideration.

December 15, 1791

Virginia becomes the 11th state to ratify the 10 amendments that will become the Bill of Rights. This gives the amendments enough support to become law.

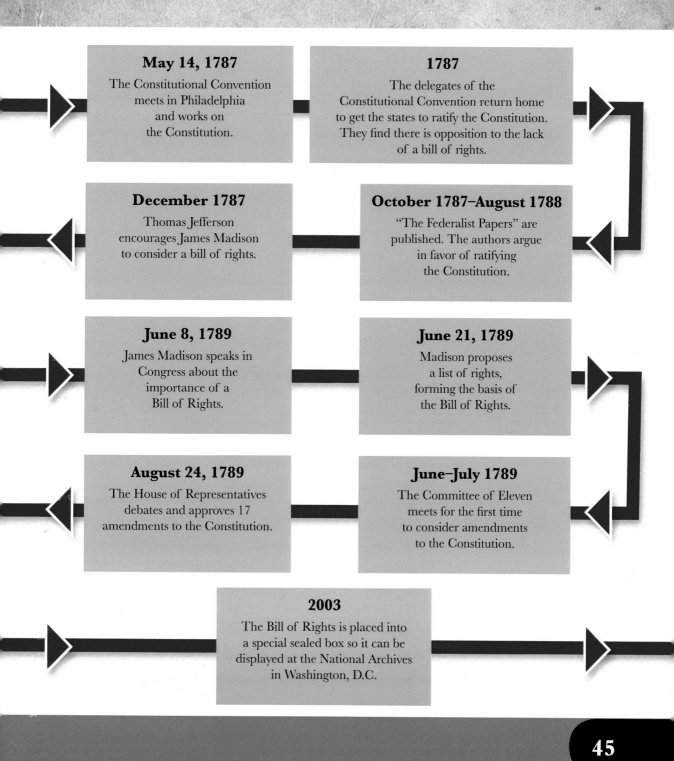

May 14, 1787

The Constitutional Convention meets in Philadelphia and works on the Constitution.

1787

The delegates of the Constitutional Convention return home to get the states to ratify the Constitution. They find there is opposition to the lack of a bill of rights.

December 1787

Thomas Jefferson encourages James Madison to consider a bill of rights.

October 1787–August 1788

"The Federalist Papers" are published. The authors argue in favor of ratifying the Constitution.

June 8, 1789

James Madison speaks in Congress about the importance of a Bill of Rights.

June 21, 1789

Madison proposes a list of rights, forming the basis of the Bill of Rights.

August 24, 1789

The House of Representatives debates and approves 17 amendments to the Constitution.

June–July 1789

The Committee of Eleven meets for the first time to consider amendments to the Constitution.

2003

The Bill of Rights is placed into a special sealed box so it can be displayed at the National Archives in Washington, D.C.

Glossary

amendment change or addition to an official document

Anti-Federalist person who did not want a strong federal government

archive place that holds historical documents and other primary sources

archivist expert who works in an archive

civil rights rights that every person should have

colonist person who lives in a colony

colony area controlled by another country

Congress legislative body of the United States, made up of the Senate and the House of Representatives

conservator expert who repairs and restores old documents

Constitution law of the United States, ratified in 1789

convention large meeting

Declaration of Independence document written by Thomas Jefferson in 1776 that proclaims freedom from Great Britain

delegate person sent to a meeting to represent others

engross to create the final version of a legal document

Federalist person who prefers a strong central government

Founding Father American leader who established the national government of the United States

House of Representatives lower branch of the Congress

parchment strong writing material, much like a piece of leather

Parliament main lawmaking body of the British government

primary source document or object made in the past that provides information about a certain time

protest to come together publicly to show disapproval of something

ratify approve

Revolutionary War war fought by American colonists from 1775 to 1783 to win independence from British rule

secondary source account written by someone who studied primary sources

Senate upper chamber of the United States Congress

Find Out More

Books

Freedman, Russell. *In Defense of Liberty: The Story of America's Bill of Rights.*
New York: Holiday House, 2003.

Sobel, Syl. *The Bill of Rights: Protecting Our Freedom Then and Now.*
Hauppauge, N.Y.: Barron's, 2008.

Stein, R. Conrad. *The National Archives.* Danbury, Conn.: Franklin Watts, 2002.

Swain, Gwenyth. *Declaring Freedom.* Minneapolis, Minn.: Lerner, 2004.

Taylor-Butler, Christine. *The Bill of Rights.* New York: Children's Press, 2008.

Websites

www.archives.gov/exhibits/charters/bill_of_rights.html
National Archives
Visit the website of the National Archives to learn more about the Bill of Rights. This site also has images of the Bill of Rights parchment.

www.billofrightsinstitute.org/page.aspx?pid=463
The Bill of Rights Institute
This website has information for students and teachers about the Bill of Rights.

http://www.loc.gov/exhibits/treasures/trt013.html
Treasures of the Library of Congress
Visit the Library of Congress website to take a closer look at important primary source documents.

Index